SPORTS ENCYCLOPEDIA

GYMNASTICS AND CYCLING SPORTS

Om KIDZ
An imprint of Om Books International

Contents

GYMNASTICS

The word "gymnastics" was derived from the common Greek word "gymnos", meaning "to exercise naked". In ancient times, male athletes exercised in an unclothed state or with minimal clothing. The place of their training came to be known as a "gymnasium".

Johann Christoph Friedrich Guts Muths and Friedrich Ludwig Jahn created various sets of exercises in the late-eighteenth and early-nineteenth century Germany. They also invented or adapted various apparatuses for the conditioning of specific sets of muscles in the human body.

Francisco Amorõs was a Spanish Colonel. He first introduced educative gymnastics in France. Between the three of them, they founded and developed the modern sports of gymnastics as it is enjoyed today.

The Federation of International Gymnastics (FIG) was founded in Liege, in 1881. Men's gymnastics became so popular that it was included in the first Modern Olympic Games in 1896. Gymnastics also gained popularity with the advent of television since its grace and show of skill made it an ideal spectator sport.

> **Did you know?** Before 2006, artistic gymnastic routines were scored on a scale of 0-10, with 10 being the highest. Nadia Comaneci scored the first perfect 10 with this system. However, in 2006, a two-part scoring system was introduced and the scores were given in grades.

Balance Beam

Balance beam is the name of a gymnastic sport as well as the apparatus on which it is performed. The beam is a thin and small plank made of leather-like material. This sport is sometimes called "beam". BB is the abbreviated name for scoring.

This gymnast is attempting a balance beam handstand. Next, she will raise her other leg in the air.

Origin

The balance beam is a women's competitive event in gymnastics. Johann Christoph Friedrich Guts Muths came up with the idea of a balance beam. He used a round pine tree trunk and laid it horizontally and proposed that a gymnast should be able to balance his/her body on it. This beam was 64-feet long. It was later called "schweben" which is the German word for "floating".

The balance beam became a part of the world championships in Budapest in 1934. These were the early days of the events featuring artistic gymnastic sports. It mostly had female participants. Balance beam initially focussed more on dance than on tumbling. Even at the Olympic level, it focussed more on dance poses and leaps.

Olga Korbut and Nadia Comaneci were among the first gymnasts in the 1970s to use a beam to display various advanced tumbling combinations and artistic aerial skills. The material of the beam changed from wood to a leather-like material to make it less slippery. As the beam became safer, other athletes started participating in the event. Today, balance beam routines still consist of a mix of acrobatic skills, dance elements, leaps and poses. Though the superficial resemblances to early balance beam routines remain, the routines themselves have to be performed with significantly greater skill.

Rules

At the international level, a beam routine must consist of:

- A connection of two dance elements, jumps or hops and one leap with legs in the 180-degree split position
- A full turn on one foot
- A series of two acrobatic skills
- Acrobatic elements in different directions performed moving sidewards, forwards and backwards
- Include a dismount from the beam

The routine may last at the most for 90 seconds. A mat or springboard may be used for the mount. Deductions are taken for all errors made while on the beam. The errors could range from a lapse in control, wobbling, stumbling and other balance checks to maintain one's balance, bad technique or its execution, inability to obtain the Code of Points allocated to each gymnast. A fall from the beam leads to an automatic deduction of one point.

The beam may have small markings to aid the gymnast. The gymnast may compete barefoot or wear special beam shoes if he/she so chooses.

The use of chalk on the hands or feet for additional stability is also permitted.

The gymnast is not allowed any form of assistance. Spotting or correction from the coach is not permitted. The coach may accompany the gymnast to the podium. But this is only in case a springboard is used so he/she may quickly remove it.

Measurements of the apparatus as published by the Fédération Internationale de Gymnastique (FIG) in the Apparatus Norms are:

- Height: 124 cm
- Length: 500 cm
- Width: 10 cm (3.9 inches)

Gymnasts make jumps, leaps, tumbles and somersaults back and forth on the beam.

The routine ends with the gymnast landing a few steps away from the other end of the beam. The gymnast takes gentle steps forward and then dismounts.

Wall of fame

Daniela Silivas is a Romanian gymnast who has won three gold, two silver and one bronze medal at the 1988 Olympic Games.

Dorina Böczögő from Hungary is a three-time gold medallist in the balance beam event of the World Cup series.

Aly Raisman was the captain of the 2012 Summer Olympics team from the USA, who went on to win the gold medal.

Fact card

- To improve one's beam skills and maintain one's balance and control, it is essential to develop a strong stomach as well as back and hip muscles.
- The origins of the balance beam as a form of dance are clear from the fact that the balance beam is exclusively a women's event.
- A thicker and lower beam approximately six inches off the ground is used by gymnasts to practice difficult tumbling passes.

Horizontal Bar

The horizontal bar, or high bar, is an apparatus used by male gymnasts in artistic gymnastics.
The gymnasts have to perform on a horizontal bar which is placed a few feet above the ground.

Origin

We can trace the origins of the horizontal bar back to ancient Greece and Rome. It was practiced through the Middle Ages by acrobats. Johann Christoph Friedrich Guts Muths introduced it as a gymnastic sport in his 1793 book "Gymnastik für die Jugend". However, the true father of the modern high bar or horizontal bar is Friedrich Ludwig Jahn. He carried out the developments and popularised the use of the horizontal bar in 1811.

The horizontal bar has been a part of artistic gymnastics since the evolution of the modern Olympics. Originally, the bar was a cylindrical metal (typically steel) bar. It was rigidly held above and parallel to the floor by a system of cables and stiff vertical supports for robustness. Today, a more elastic fiberglass core rail is used in the higher levels of competitions.

Though it is a men's event, in smaller competitions, women also perform on the horizontal bar.

Equipment

The dimensions of the horizontal bar are clearly fixed and defined. They are specified in FIG's Apparatus Norms brochure as:

- Height: 278 cm (including about 30 cm landing mats)
- Length: 240 cm
- Diameter of the bar: 2.8 cm

There are several grips that the players use to hold onto the horizontal bar. It is important to maintain a good grip for safety reasons.

All gymnasts need to wear leather grips made of suede in order to have a tight grip on the bar. The bar is typically made of steel or some other form of metal.

Fact card

- The horizontal bar is an exciting and much loved spectator sport due to the aerial acrobatics involved.

A Code of Points regulates the horizontal bar. This specifically refers to the gymnastic elements used. A bar routine is a sequence of several bar skills. These include:

- Giants using various grips like overgrip, reverse grip, dorsal grip, mixed grip
- In-bar work
- Turns
- Release and regrasp skills
- A dismount

The overhand grip is also called the regular grip. It is a standard grip technique where the gymnast's hands curl around the bar in such a way that the backs of his/her hands are facing him/her. The reverse grip is the opposite of the overhand grip. Here, the gymnast's palms face him/her. In the mixed grip, the gymnast uses a combination of overhand and underhand grips with one hand in each position.

The dorsal grip is an overhand grip technique where the gymnast's legs pass through the arms. It is used to perform full body swings.

Parallel Bars

Parallel bars is a gymnastic sport which is named after the apparatus used in it. It is an artistic gymnastics event. Invented by Friedrich Ludwig Jahn in Berlin, it tests the skills and strength of the gymnast.

Origin

Friedrich Ludwig Jahn invented the parallel bars or "barren" in Berlin. "Barren" is simply the German word for bars. The first mention of parallel bars dates back to 1819, where transportable parallel bars were described. Hermann Otto Kluge is credited with creating the first set of adjustable parallel bars in 1856 in Germany.

He nested a set of tubes inside one another so they could slide around each other. The parallel bars have been part of the Olympic programme for gymnastics since the first modern Olympic games. They were an Olympic Medal Sport right since the first games in 1896.

A gymnast performs a handstand on the parallel bars using an overhand grip technique to grip the bars.

Equipment

Parallel bars are the apparatus which consist of two parallel bars that are elevated above the floor by a metal framework which provides support and rigidity to the gymnast. The bars are either made of wood or synthetic core, with a wooden outer layer. The vertical members of the supporting framework are adjustable. The distance between the bars is also adjustable. Every gymnast may vary these according to their personal preference.

The dimensions are as follows:

- Bar length: 350 cm ± 1 cm
- Bar rounded profile: 5 cm ± 1 mm vertical by 4 cm ± 1 mm horizontal
- Bar width: 4 cm ± 1 mm
- Height of bar from floor: 200 cm ± 1 cm
- Distance between bars: 42 cm ± 52 cm (adjustable)

At the international level, a routine in this event should contain at least one element from all element groups:

- Elements in support or through support
- Elements starting in the upper arm position
- Long swings in hang, face on 1 or 2 rails
- Underswings
- Dismounts

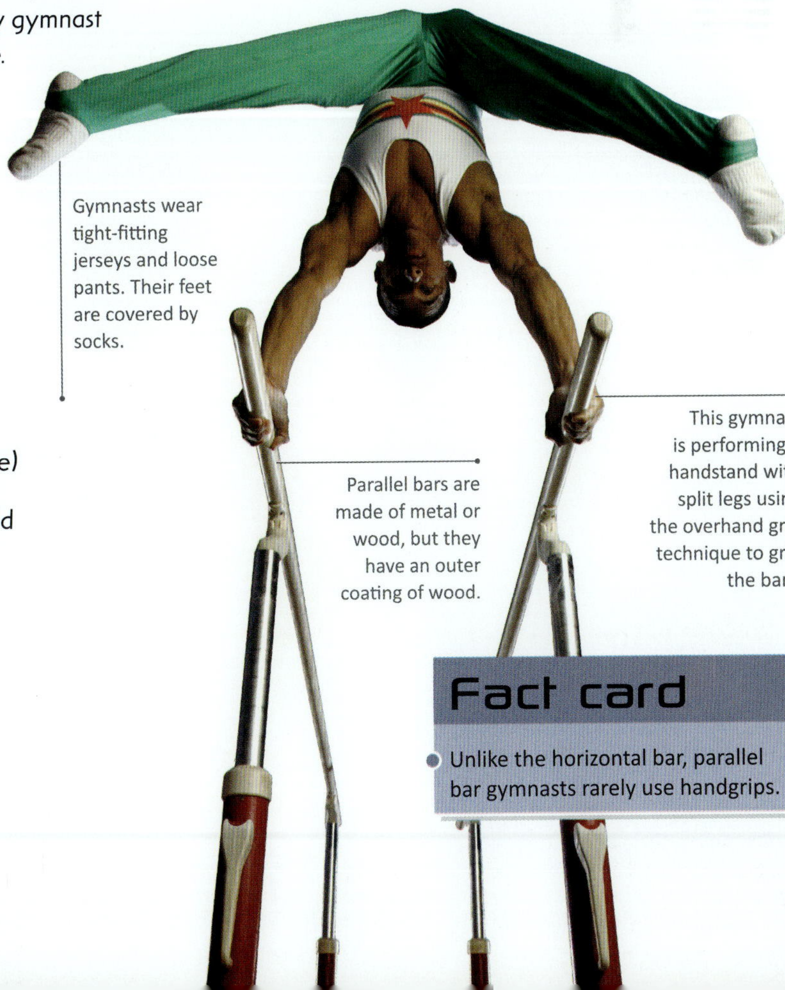

Gymnasts wear tight-fitting jerseys and loose pants. Their feet are covered by socks.

Parallel bars are made of metal or wood, but they have an outer coating of wood.

This gymnast is performing a handstand with split legs using the overhand grip technique to grip the bars.

Fact card

- Unlike the horizontal bar, parallel bar gymnasts rarely use handgrips.

Pommel Horse

Another type of gymnastic apparatus used during gymnastic competitions is the pommel horse. Also referred to as the 'side horse', it is usually used only by male gymnasts.

Single legwork refers to scissoring actions. This gymnast is performing a single legwork routine.

Origin

While most gymnastic sports are fairly recent, the pommel horse event is one of the oldest gymnastic routines that exist today. It was developed more than 600 years ago. The pommel horse probably originated in ancient Greece. It was not invented as a gymnastic routine, but rather as a way for soldiers to practice how to mount and dismount a horse without actually coming into contact with a horse. So, artificial horses were created for this purpose.

Soon, soldiers began to compete with one another to show off their skills in mounting and dismounting this artificial horse. It spread to the public and people began to perform tricks and stunts on the horse. Friedrich Ludwig Jahn is believed to have adapted this sport to fit a gymnastics routine. He trained gymnasts at it in the early 1800s. A typical modern pommel horse exercise involves both single legwork and double legwork routines.

Equipment

The Fédération Internationale de Gymnastique (FIG), in the Apparatus Norms brochure, defines the dimensions of parallel bars as:

- Height from top surface to floor: 115 cm ± 1 cm
- Length at top: 160 cm ± 1 cm
- Length at bottom: 155 cm ± 1 cm
- Width at top: 35 cm ± 1 cm
- Width at bottom: 30 cm ± 1 cm
- Height of the pommels: 12 cm ± 0.5 cm
- Distance between the pommels: 40 cm ± 45 cm (adjustable)

Pommel horse is one of the most difficult gymnastic events. It focuses less on style and more on the use of the horse, and the level of balance and strength displayed by the participants. However, at the same time, pommel horse is about technique over muscle. The routines are done with the shoulder muscles and need to be held for some time. No other routine has so much focus on the hold.

International level routines are defined. They require at least one element of each:

- Single leg swings and scissor work
- Different categories of circles and flairs (circles with legs straddled), with or without spindles and handstands
- Side and cross support travels along the length of the horse
- Kehrswings, wendeswings, flops and combined elements
- Dismounts

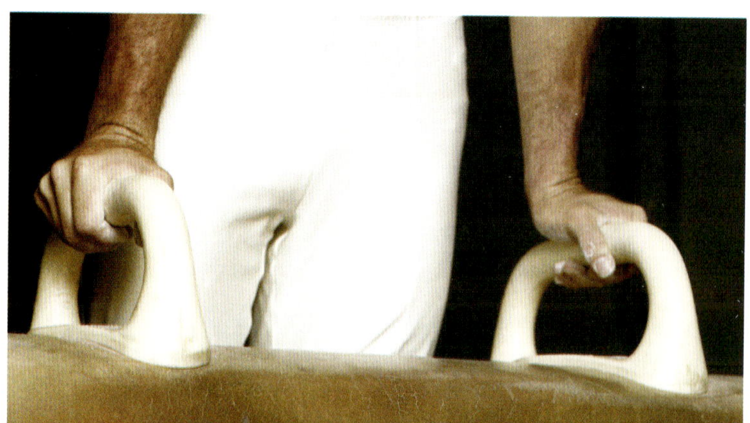

A gymnast gripping the handles of the horse, probably getting ready to dismount.

Fact card

- Alexander the Great of Macedonia is believed to have used a pommel horse for training.

Uneven Bars

Uneven bars is an artistic gymnastics event and also the name of the apparatus used. At a competition level, only women participate in this sport.

The gymnast in this picture is chalking up her hands and the equipment to avoid sweat or moisture from affecting her grip.

Origin

Earlier, the apparatus used in the parallel bars event was placed on different heights. The bars were also placed very close together at the time. As a result, gymnasts could transition from one to the other easily.

In the late 1950s, the trend shifted towards fluid motion and release moves also came into play. This is the first-known instance where manufacturers started manufacturing the bars that we see today.

Gymnasts and coaches began experimenting with different elements of the sport with specialised equipment. They began attempting more challenging dismounts by adapting moves from the men's horizontal bar event. By the mid-1980s, routines were mostly based on swing and release moves. As a result, the bars were moved even further apart. The uneven bars that are used today are also thinner than the originals so that they can be easily gripped. The modern form of the game is an Olympic sport exclusively for women.

Equipment

In the current form, the FIG defines the dimensions of the uneven bar apparatus as given below.

Height:

- Upper bar: 250 cm
- Lower bar: 170 cm
- Diameter of bar: 4 cm
- Length of the bars: 240 cm
- Diagonal distance between the two bars: 130 cm–180 cm (adjustable)

International Routines must contain one each of the following elements:

- Flight element from high bar to low bar and vice versa
- Flight element on the same bar
- At least two different grips with a close bar circle element
- Non-flight with a turn on the bar
- Dismount

The lifting of a gymnast onto a bar is not permitted as the bars are not strong enough for that.

The use of handguards and grips is permitted, as is the taping or chalking of the apparatus.

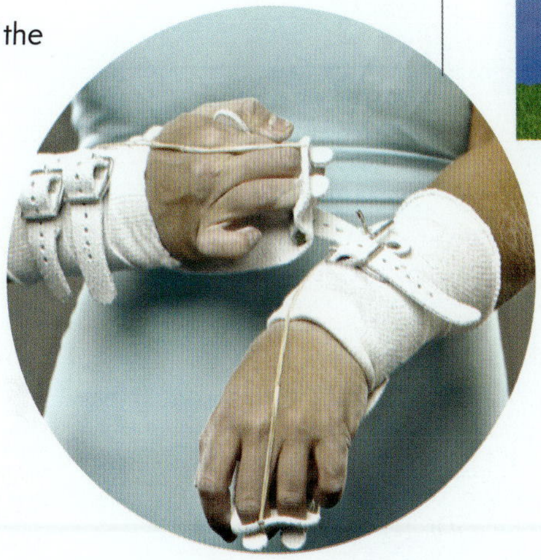

Fact card

- Coaches are allowed to catch a gymnast falling off the bars during her routine. However, she must restart the routine within 30 seconds.

Still Rings

"Still rings" is an artistic gymnastic event that is performed by men. For this routine, the gymnast must have good upper body strength to perform exercises on a pair of rings suspended from the ceiling.

This gymnast is performing an L-sit swing routine on the rings.

Gymnasts may opt out of wearing gloves to get a better grip of the rings.

Origin

Friedrich Jahn invented still rings or "static rings" in the early nineteenth century. It was initially developed to increase the upper body strength amongst gymnasts. Since the 1960s, swinging has become more prominent in competitive routines. This has reduced the strength demanded of gymnasts. Competitive exercise on the rings must be performed with the rings held in a completely stationary position. The rings must not swing or move like a pendulum.

Equipment

The FIG norms define the dimensions of the rings and their location as:

- Inner diameter: 18 cm ± 0.1 cm
- Distance from point of attachment to lower inner side of the rings: 300 cm ± 1 cm
- Distance between two points of attachment: 50 cm ± 0.5 cm

If gymnasts bend their arms during the strength rounds, their points will be deducted from the total.

Fact card

- Rings are used in physical therapy and various other fitness regimes. In non-competitive environments, men and women have equal participation for this sport.

Exercises have the swing, strength and hold routines. The swing, the held handstand, the static strength hold and the aerial dismount must be fulfilled in a still ring routine. The international routines must contain elements from each of the following groups:

- Kip and swing elements (including an L-sit)
- Swings to handstand
- Swings to strength hold elements (not L-sits)
- Strength elements and hold elements
- Dismounts

The Code of Points applies to rings in the same way as to other gymnastics. Deductions are made from the total score of a gymnast if he is seen using straps or cables to maintain his balance on the rings or during a hold move.

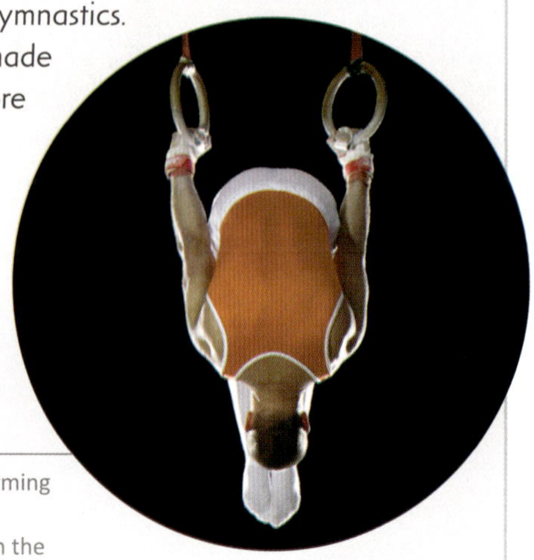

This gymnast is performing a total body swing by gripping the rings with the underhand technique.

Vault

A vault, commonly known as a "vaulting horse", is a gymnastic sport for both genders. It is much like a pommel horse with some minor differences in construction.

The gymnast has taken a leap off of the vault and is set to land on the mat.

Origin

Friedrich Ludwig Jahn invented the vaulting horse in the early 1800s. It was developed for similar reasons as the pommel horse equipment. However, it was constructed without the handles seen on the pommel horse. The sport was designed for both women and men. However, men had to vault the horse along its length while women did it along its width.

The vaulting horse equipment was used from the beginning of the modern games which started in 1896. However, there were a number of accidents leading up to the 2000 Olympics. Many gymnasts were hurt, including two who suffered paralysis, with one fatality. The modern Olympic games use a vaulting table instead.

Equipment

The new vault dimensions as specified are:

- Length: 120 cm ± 1 cm
- Width: 95 cm ± 1 cm

Height:

- Men: 135 cm ± 1 cm
- Women: 125 cm ± 1 cm

Run-up area:

- Length: 2,500 cm ± 10 cm
- Width: 100 cm ± 1 cm

This gymnast has landed on the vault. Next, the gymnast will leap off and land on the mat with both hands.

This is the new vaulting table. The old vaulting table was slippery and caused several accidents.

Gymnasts run along the run-up area of the vault. Then, they hop off the springboard. They push off the vault with their hands to land on the table. While the gymnasts are still in the air, they perform acrobatic tricks with their hands, legs and torso. Deductions are made for hops, restoring balance or any deviation from form.

Fact card

- Dutch gymnastics equipment company Janssen-Fritsen has been making the vaulting table since the 1990s. It has a flatter surface with more area to perform tricks.
- Gymnasts have nicknamed the new vaulting table as "the tongue".

Floor Gymnastics

Floor exercises and tumbling have long been a part of many courtly traditions. The jester or tumbler would often perform acrobatics along with juggling tricks. Floor gymnastics also has a much more recent modern usage.

Origin

The floor, in this instance, refers to a specially prepared exercise surface. This is considered an apparatus, and is used by both female and male gymnasts. A spring floor is used in most competitive gymnastics to provide bounce. Unlike the ones used sometimes in cheerleading, the spring floor is used for indoor athletics and is designed to reduce bounce.

The floor apparatus originated as a "free exercise" for men. Although very similar to the floor exercise of today, it wasn't practiced as a competitive sport. It was used purely for practice. It was only in 1948 that women were allowed to compete on the floor. Finally, the floor exercise was introduced as an individual Olympic medal sport for men in 1936 and women in 1952. Today, the floor gymnastic routines are conducted on spring floors.

The spring floors contain a combination of springs and rubber foam on plywood floors, which makes the surface bouncy. This is extremely necessary to enable the gymnasts to gain height while tumbling. It is also a safety measure.

Form is a very important element of the floor gymnastics routines.

The quality of the entire performance depends upon the use of the floor, form and acrobatic movements.

The gymnasts are expected to perform rhythmic and harmonious movements using the entire floor.

A gymnast's points are cut if she does not use the floor properly.

Rules

The floor exercise area is the same for men and women. The Fédération Internationale de Gymnastique (FIG) in the Apparatus Norms brochure publishes measurements of the floor exercise apparatus.

They are currently as follows:

- Performance area: 1,200 cm x 1,200 cm ± 3 cm
- Diagonals: 1,697 cm ± 5 cm
- Border: 100 cm
- Safety zone: 200 cm

Within the given time, the gymnasts must perform all the compulsory routines that are given in the regulations.

The main differences between the routines for men and women are that the men's routines must last for 50–70 seconds as opposed to those for women, which must last for 70–90 seconds. Also, men are not allowed to use music as an accompaniment, whereas it is compulsory for women.

This gymnast is performing a floor exercise. Next, she will plant her feet on the ground and stand.

The compulsory routines are as follows:

For men:

- Non-acrobatic elements
- Acrobatic elements forward
- Acrobatic elements backward
- Acrobatical elements sideways, backward jumps with half turns, salto forward, backward jumps with a quarter turn and a side flip (side sami)

For women:

- Connection of two dance elements (one must be a 180-degree split)
- Saltos forward/sideways and backward
- Double saltos
- Saltos with a minimum of one full twist
- D+ dismount

The women's routine is choreographed in advance, and is composed of acrobatic and dance elements. The men's routine includes both the acrobatic as well as gymnastic elements like balance, strength and flexibility.

The routine must be choreographed for form with a harmonious rhythmic exercise using the whole floor area. As with other gymnastic events, scores are based on difficulty, form and overall performance quality.

This young gymnast is performing an acrobatic element in her routine.

Just like in other gymnastic events, even in floor gymnastics, the participants must maintain their form.

Wall of fame

Anna Pavlova is a Russian gymnast who performs artistic and floor gymnastics. She is known for her balletic style and clean movements. She has been named as one of the most talented gymnasts of the decade.

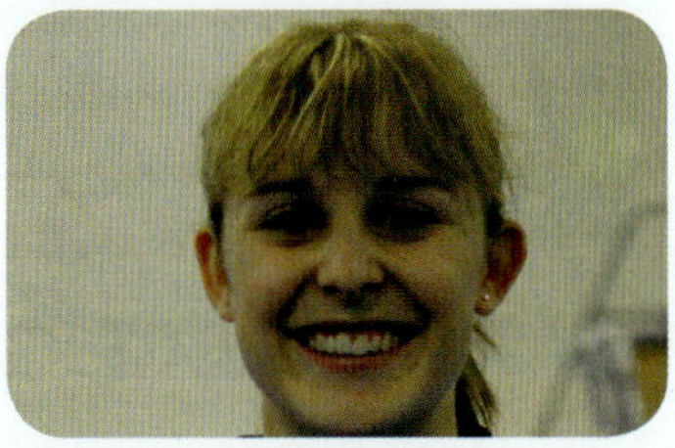

Lauren Mitchell is an Australian floor and artistic gymnast who won the 2010 World Championship for her routine.

Shannon Miller won the gold medal for her floor routines at the 1993 World Championships.

Fact card

- The music used in the women's floor exercises may be of any known musical style and played with any instrument. However, it may not include spoken words or sung lyrics of any kind. Points are penalised for lyrics.
- The English abbreviation for the event in gymnastics scoring is FX.
- There are many professional gymnastic choreographers, such as Lisa Luke (USA), Adriana Pop (Romania, France, China), Nancy Roche (USA) and Geza Pozar (Romania).

Rhythmic Gymnastics

Rhythmic gymnastics originated from the idea of expression through movements. It is a group of sports which is combination of dance, apparatus manipulation, ballet and gymnastics.

Along with speed and agility, the form of a gymnast needs to be correct at all times.

Gymnasts do not hold poses for too long as their routine needs to look quick and sharp.

The ball used in this routine is light enough to carry and roll on the body.

Young girls and women below the age of 24 perform this event.

Origin

Jean-Georges Noverre (1722–1810), François Delsarte (1811–1871) and Rudolf Bode (1881–1970) are thought to be the originators of rhythmic gymnastics. The nineteenth century Swedish system of free exercise created by Peter Henry Ling, further developed this idea. Eurythmics was another system invented in the 1880s.

Émile Jaques-Dalcroze of Switzerland created a form of physical training for musicians and dancers. George Demeny of France also created certain exercises which he set to music. His intention was to encourage good posture, grace and muscular flexibility in gymnasts. The 1900s saw the combination of all these styles. A school of rhythmic gymnastics was started in Sweden. Ernst Idla of Estonia established a degree of difficulty for each movement as the basis of judgement and comparison. Hinrich Medau founded The Medau School to train gymnasts in these "modern gymnastics" in Berlin in 1929.

In the 1940s, Soviet Russia saw the rise of competitive gymnastics. FIG formally recognised this discipline in 1961. At first it was termed "modern gymnastics", then termed as "rhythmic sportive gymnastics", and finally the current name of "rhythmic gymnastics" emerged. Budapest saw the first instance of World Championships for individual rhythmic gymnasts in 1963. The same level for groups started in Copenhagen, Denmark in 1967. In 1984, at the Los Angeles Summer Olympics, rhythmic gymnastics were held for the first time. It had an Individual All-Around competition. As of 1996, the group competition was also held in the Olympics.

At the Olympic level, rhythmic gymnastics is held only for female participants. They can participate in the olympic games and other international competitions starting from 1st January of their sixteenth year.

Rules

Rhythmic gymnastics is carried out with five apparatuses. Out of these, the Federation Internationale de Gymnastique (FIG) allows only four at any point of time. For example, up to 2010, clubs were not used at the senior level. Group and senior level were not allowed rope from 2011 to 2015. Various apparatuses are allowed.

Ball

It is a sphere which might be made of rubber or a synthetic material (pliable plastic) provided it possesses the same elasticity as rubber. It ranges from 18 to 20 cm in diameter and must weigh at least 400 g. The ball is to be held in the hand. It may not rest against the wrist or be grasped in any way. The gymnast must use both hands to perform a routine consisting of throwing, bouncing or rolling. The whole floor area must be utilised whilst showing continuous flowing movement. The ball serves to emphasise the gymnast's flowing lines and the level of difficulty of the manoeuvring techniques used.

Hoop

A hoop is a ring with an interior diameter of 51–90 cm. It can be made of plastic or wood but must weigh at least 300 g and retain its shape during the routine. A hoop routine must include rotation around the hand or body and rolling on the floor with the hoop. It must also include swings, circles, throws, passes through and over the hoop. Both apparatus handling skill and body difficulty like leaps, jumps and pivots are present in hoop routines.

This gymnast is using the hoop as a part of her routine. It is a perfect routine for children because of their short height.

Gymnasts popularly choose sequins for their costumes.

Gymnasts wear colourful and designed costumes and ensure that their apparatuses match, or contrast with their suits.

Most participants wear ballet shoes. Routines are inspired from ballet moves.

Wall of fame

Janine Murray won the gold medal for the team event in rhythmic gymnastics in the 2010 Commonwealth Games.

Inna Zhukova won the silver medal in the 2008 Olympics for the All-around routine.

Maria Gigova is a three-time winner of the World All-around championship contests.

Fact card

- Many state federations had been forced to boycott the 1984 Olympics due to the influence of the Soviet Union. At this time, the Eastern Bloc nations dominated the sport. As a result of their boycott, the sport saw relatively little participation.
- A gymnast born on 31st December, 2000, would not be eligible for the 2016 Olympics, but one born on 1st January, 2001, would be.
- Spain and Italy focus more on the group gymnastics event rather than individual events.

Ribbon

The ribbon must be made of satin or a similar cloth. The ribbon itself must be at least 35 g and 4–6 cm in width, with a minimum length of 6 m for seniors and 5 m for juniors.

The ribbon is affixed to the stick through a supple attachment like a thread, nylon cord or a series of articulated rings. Compulsory elements for the ribbon include flicks, circles, snakes, spirals and throws.

A high degree of co-ordination is necessary to form the spirals and circles as any knots that may accidentally form in the ribbon will be penalised.

Large, smooth and flowing movements are desired in the routine.

Ribbon gymnastics is so popular that even dancers incorporate it into their dance routines.

In rhythmic gymnastics, there are group and individual events. In a group event, the gymnasts must coordinate the colour, cut and style of their clothes. They must ensure that their physical coordination is also up to the mark. Not moving in synchronisation is one of the major factors of losing points in a match.

Another important factor to remember is that all gymnasts should have the correct number of equipment, and all the equipment should meet the conditions set by the regulating bodies.

Every professional and non-professional platform has rules for the equipment, clothes and sets.

In group competitions, gymnasts must be of a similar age.

Clubs look similar to bowling pins but are made entirely of plastic.

Some gymnasts use clubs that are made of wood.

Clubs

The club is built along an internal rod. A handle made of polyolefin plastic is wrapped on its base so that some airspace is formed between it and the core. This makes the club softer on the hands.

Clubs are made in various lengths, generally ranging from 400 to 530 mm. The basic form requires that each club is rotated once per throw. Initially the handle moves down and away from the throwing hand. Double and triple spins are also regularly performed. These allow the club to be thrown higher for more advanced patterns and allow tricks like 360-degree turns to be performed underneath.

Wall of fame

Aliya Garayeva won the 2007 European Championships for the use of rope in rhythmic gymnastics.

Yulia Raskina won the 1999 World Championships in the ribbon round.

Maria Petrova won the 1995 World Championships for the clubs round.

Rope

The fundamental requirements of a rope routine include leaps and skipping. Swings, throws, circles, rotations and figures of eight are also commonly used.

The rope may be made of hemp or a synthetic material. It must be light and supple. The length is such that when the rope is held underneath a gymnast's foot, the ends reach her armpits.

These rhythmic gymnastic routines are judged on two criterias: difficulty and execution of the routine. There is a 20-point scale for each event, currently.

The gymnast with the most points wins the competition. The points are also scored in grades in some other types of competition. In the grading system, the A grade goes to the performance and the B grade on minor points of the performance.

The length of the rope depends on the height of the gymnast.

Gymnasts need to be aware of the movement of the rope as they might be injured by it.

Acrobatics

Acrobatics as a sport displays skill, strength and grace. Acrobatics is an umbrella term and involves the use of various apparatuses.

Origin

Acrobatic traditions are found in many cultures. Minoan art from circa 2000 BCE contained depictions of acrobatic feats on the backs of bulls. Ancient Greek and Roman cultures had acrobatic displays. Even the European courts in the Middle Ages had a court jester who would perform acrobatics. The term "acrobat" originated from the Greek word "akrobate" meaning "to walk on tiptoe or strut".

In China, acrobatics have been a part of the culture since the Western Han Dynasty (206 BCE–220 CE). Court displays were held through the seventh and tenth century in the reign of the Tang Dynasty.

Acrobats wear spandex or clothes made of lycra.

Acrobats practice how to hold certain positions and also move with fluidity.

Acrobats are extremely flexible and supple.

Quick transitional movement is the most important feature of acrobatic sports.

A duo performs an acrobatic dance for the judges. Even non-competitive acrobatic performances follow certain guidelines.

Fact card

- Traditionally, acrobatic skills were kept within families and were passed on from generation to generation.
- Acrobatics are commonly used in gymnastics as well as martial arts. Certain moves in wing chun and kung fu are excellent examples of acrobatics.

In 1859, Charles Blondin crossed the Niagara Falls on a tightrope and rekindled public interest in aerial gymnasts and acrobats.

The Scheffers, Craggs, Hanlon-Voltas, Sandow, Lauck, Fox, Cinquevalli, Caicedo and the Potters were the most prominent acrobats in Europe and the USA around 1900.

Modern form

Modern acrobatics are performed with the use of apparatus, such as poles, one-wheel cycles, balls, barrels, tightropes, trampolines and flying trapezes.

The Concellos and Codonas made the flying trapeze famous. Juggler Enrico Rastelli captivated the audience with his skills. The Wallendas, a family originally from Germany, became famous wire artists.

Today, acrobatics are performed in fairgrounds, circuses and theatres. They account for some of the most beautiful performances in the world.

Sports Aerobics

Aerobics is a form of workout in which different body muscles are exercised through routines, with minimal use of external implements. They were developed primarily as a means of attaining overall body fitness and flexibility. Eventually, the exercise form was adapted into a sport, known as sports aerobics.

Origin

Aerobics has been a popular form of physical training for people since many decades. This form of exercise has been in the mainstream since the mid-1970s. This was also the time when it was invented and introduced to the public.

It was first converted into a sport discipline in the late 1980s. It became truly competitive when the first official World Championship was held in 1995 in Paris.

There were 34 participating member nations in this sport. The International World Games Association included the sport of aerobics in the fifth World Games in 1997. It has remained a part of it ever since. Sports aerobics has not been included in the Olympics yet. However, it has been recognised as a gymnastic discipline by the FIG.

Aerobics is also done with the help of the medicine ball, as seen in this picture.

Gameplay

The performance area is a square that measures 7 m ×7 m. Performers compete in divisions as follows:

- Junior divisions (primary and secondary teams)
- Novice divisions (including individual men and women)
- Intermediate divisions (comprising individual men and women)
- Mixed pairs and trios
- Elite divisions (including individual men and women, mixed pairs and trios)

Aerobics consist of the elements of dynamic strength, static strength, jumps and leaps (power), kicks, balance and flexibility.

Aerobics is also performed by lying on the floor and moving the arms and legs.

The use of light weights and dumbells has been introduced to make the routines tougher.

Fact card

- The costume for sports aerobics is specific and consists of a one-piece leotard, shimmer tan tights, white socks and white runners. Performers wear their hair in a tight bun if they have long hair. Women wear unitards and men wear lycra shirts and spandex.

Trapeze

The flying trapeze is a type of equipment often related to circuses. Acrobats are seen jumping from platforms holding on to horizontal bars suspended with two ropes from the roof. Over the years, people took it up as a sport that involves tumbling and gliding through the air on momentum alone. This sport called "trapeze" is a fairly modern sport and is extremely beautiful to watch.

Origin

Trapeze was originally a French art. It was invented in the mid-1800s in Toulouse. A young man by the name of Jules Leotard is credited with the invention of the trapeze.

Techniques

Typically, trapeze is performed on a short horizontal bar which is hung by ropes or metal straps from a support on the ceiling. Commonly found in circus performances, the trapeze is an aerial apparatus. Trapeze may be performed solo, in pairs, in threes or as a group act.

- **Static trapeze:** The performer performs stunts around a static bar and ropes.
- **Swinging trapeze:** This is an act which is performed on a trapeze by swinging in a forward and backward motion.
- **Flying trapeze:** The performer or the "flyer" grabs the trapeze bar and jumps off a high platform. The swing is created with the smart knowledge of gravity.

The performer often releases the bar, only to be caught by another performer or the "catcher", who hangs by the knees on another trapeze. Flying trapeze is generally performed over a net for safety reasons.

Trapeze performers position their legs and hands gracefully at all times.

In competitive performances, it is important for the performers to have proper form at all times.

- **Washington trapeze:** It refers to a variation on static and swinging trapeze where the aerialist performs various types of headstands on the bar. It is typically much heavier than a normal trapeze bar and has a small round headstand. Wires are used instead of ropes as the trapeze is raised and lowered and lifted during the performance.
- **Dance trapeze:** It refers to a form of aerial dance on a trapeze. The ropes of the trapeze are often attached to a single swivel, which allows the trapeze to spin in either small or large circles.
- **Double trapeze**: It is a variation on the static trapeze in which two performers work together on the same trapeze. In case the performers are swinging, it is called a swinging double trapeze.
- **Multiple trapeze**: It refers to a number of different shapes and sizes of trapezes. This includes double, triple and much larger multiple trapezes. Multiple flyers use these trapezes simultaneously.

Trapeze is such a popular and captivating performance that its influence has slipped into other forms of art. This art that requires a lot of grace and form, has to be performed with a clear mind, agility and extremely quick reflexes. The trapeze has gone through a lot of transformations from its early beginnings. Mattresses that were used by Leotard for his first performance have been replaced by safety nets.

Several music videos have shown trapeze artists to add drama to the performance.

Wall of fame

The Flying Wallendas were a circus troupe who performed dangerous and daredevil stunts. They were excellent trapeze performers. They incorporated several gymnastic routines into their performances.

Karl Wallenda, born in Magdeburg, Germany, in 1905, started performing at the circus in which his family performed, at the age of six. In 1922, using all of his experience, he formed an act with his brothers, Herman and Joseph, and a young girl named Helen Kreis (whom he later married).

They toured Europe for many years and made a name for themselves. During a performance in Cuba, they were hired by John Ringling, co-founder of the very famous Ringling Brothers Circus. They got their name when the entire group fell during a performance, but with so much grace that the audience felt they were all flying.

Fact card

- The "Double Trapeze" is also referred to as the "French Trapeze".
- Jules Leotard would practice trapeze over his father's swimming pool.
- The trapeze bar is weighted and often has cable inside the supporting ropes, which gives extra strength to withstand the dynamic forces of the swing.
- Most people with good health can perform the basic moves of trapeze. But true mastery can only be gained through practice.

Trampolining

A trampoline is a device used for jumping and tumbling. It comprises a frame over which a taut piece of material such as a canvas is stretched and usually connected to the frame by cords or springs. Today, trampoline jumping is a widely practiced sport. It is considered to be an excellent mixture of classical gymnastics and modern expressionism.

Origin

Trampolining is a fairly ancient sport. The Inuit practiced a version of it, and medieval Europe had a game, in which people were tossed into the air with the help of a blanket. Although these are not the true antecedents of the modern sport of trampoline, they indicate that the concept had been around for some time.

George Nissen and Larry Griswold built the first modern trampoline in the 1930s. The name came from the Spanish word "trampolín" meaning the "diving board". Trapeze artists, who used a tight net to bounce off for entertainment and safety, had inspired the two inventors.

Trampoline was initially a trademarked name for the concept of a "rebound tumbler". However, since then, it has lost that status, and has now become a generic trademark. Trampolining became an Olympic sport in 2000.

It is an excellent form of exercise for all children and teenagers.

Performers perform stunts like wheelies, rolls, jumps and splits on the trampoline.

While starting off, people repeatedly bounce on the trampoline to create momentum and height.

Rules

Trampolining routines consist of 10 contacts with the trampoline bed. These are a combination of varying rotations, twists and shapes, with take-off and landing. The contact points allowed are: feet, back, front and seat.

The routine should start and end on the feet, and should commence within 60 seconds of entry. Trampolines used in competitions must have their springs covered in pads to reduce the chance of injury when landing off the bed. End decks must also be padded, since they are the most common locations to fall off from.

The cloth of the trampoline is not elastic, but its bounce comes from the springs that tightly connect it to the frame.

Fact card

- The Inuit would toss each other into the air on a walrus skin in a game called "nalukataq", which is very similar to a trampoline.
- Blanket tossing was a form of vigilante punishment in Europe. Instances of these are seen in Wakefield Second Shepherds' Play and *'Don Quixote'*.

CYCLING SPORTS

Cycles are used as a means of transport and even for recreation. They have been in existence for more than a century and half. The most popular bicycles have evolved from different designs, such as the distinctive penny-farthing velocipede and now, the modern bicycle. The less common cycles are the unicycle, the tricycle and the quadricycle.

With time, this means of transport became a competitive sport. Today, people all around the world compete in cycling races. Generally, cycling sports do not just mean the normal two-wheeler. They include all kinds of cycles. Cycling sports are carried out in a variety of terrain from paved roads to arenas and mountain paths. Depending on the terrain and the type of bicycle used, cycling sports can be divided into various categories. There are certain cycling sports that focus on stunts and skills rather than speed.

Cycling events are not as popular as other kinds of sports, but there are certain cycling events that have huge followers, irrespective of whether they like cycling or not. The *Tour de France* is one such cycling event that people all around the world look forward to.

▸ **Did you know?** The tight clothing worn by professional cyclists helps them ride a cycle for long hours. The shorts have an extra padding or "chamois" to make sitting on a cycle for long hours comfortable.

Road Bicycle Racing

All cyclists wear light helmets on their heads. These are strapped to their chin.

Bicycle racing is a sport usually carried out over long distances, often on paved roads. The roads are smooth and long-running. Road bicycle racing is a popular event with races like Tour de France having a high viewership.

Origin

Road bicycle racing is the oldest form of cycle racing competition. In the beginning, people reported many injuries. Slowly, safety measures were developed. At one time, it was the most popular sport in the USA. The quad bike, which is the most common type of cycle, was invented in 1899. By this time, bicycle tracks had also come into use. But road bicycle racing always had greater appeal for cyclists than track racing. Long-distance pavement races were introduced later. It further developed the sport of cycling. People also began cycling for charity. The sport today is safer and uses more safety precautions than the old-time cycling sport.

Cycling marathons are held for non-professional cyclists who enjoy cycling or look at it as a form of exercise.

Fact card

- The wheel has a diameter of around 55–70 cm.
- Professional cyclists shave off their body hair so that they can dust off the gravel or small stones that might stick to them during injuries. They also need to do this to be able to apply ointments easily.

Types of races

Road bicycle races are of various kinds, from one-day events to marathons. The distance of a one-day race can vary from 5 km to more than 200 km. It can also be a destination-based event where the participants need to follow a map and reach a certain point. It might also be a lap-based event which requires the participants to take laps on a track.

"Criteriums" are races over a small town or circuit. In case of individual trailed races, each player starts at a different point, covering the same distance to reach a common destination. There is a fixed time limit to this type of race. Those who don't finish within the time limit are disqualified.

In stage races, the different stages of the race run consecutively. The staged races that last about three weeks or more are called "grand tours". Tour de France is a world famous cycling event. Ultra marathon races have a clocked time from start to finish. They are usually long distance races.

Track Cycling

Track cycling is a bicycle racing sport which is held on tracks built specially for cyclists. The stadiums that house these special tracks are called "velodromes".

This cyclist is moving on an indoor track. He is riding a lightweight cycle.

Origin

Track cycling started gaining popularity as early as 1870. Smaller, indoor velodromes were built at that time. These are similar to modern velodromes. They had straight tracks with slightly banked turns.

Indoor tracks are better for spectators as this allows them to view the entire race themselves. The invention of lightweight cycles revolutionised this sport.

This sport has always been a part of the Olympics. However, the womens' cycling tournament was only introduced recently as a new category in the races.

Types of races

There are various formats of indoor racing. The major events are sprint, team sprint, keirin and timed trail. All of these races fall in the speed or sprint category.

The riders, who are a part of any one category, usually do not perform in the other category as the training for each of these categories is different. The sprint races focus on raw speed and control. They last for about 8–10 laps.

The endurance and ultra-endurance races require different training as the cyclists are expected to race for nearly 4828 km in the latter category. They might also be expected to complete the race in laps. There is an individual pursuit, team pursuit, scratch race and point's race division in the endurance races. Each race can last more than 12–16 laps, and can go up to 200 laps as well.

Helmets are a must in all cycling events. There are set rules for the size and weight of the helmet.

Cyclists need to follow rules and regulations with regard to the size and weight of the bicycle.

Fact card

- The bicycles used for racing were initially called "velocipedes".
- Pneumatic tyres provided greater speed and also allowed for a better brake system.
- Race Across America is a three-decade old racing competition which needs to be completed in 12 days.

Bicycle Motocross

Bicycle motocross is a cross between road bicycle racing and motocross racing. It is a cycle sport which is performed on BMX cycles. It combines racing with stunts. It is also known as off-road bicycle racing.

Origin

This game was introduced in the early 1970s in Southern California. It used smaller and lighter cycles because people wanted to improve their performance.

The cycles were modified. The races were also of a slightly different format as they included the use of stunts along with racing. This increased the popularity of the event. Around the mid-1970s, this kind of racing became hugely popular.

The national bicycle league was inaugurated in 1974. The first Bicycle Motocross World Championship was held in 1982. This event is included in the Summer Olympics.

Cyclists must wear gloves to grip the handle better.

This cyclist is performing a wheelie. This is a special cycling stunt.

The pedals are heavier and harder than in normal cycles.

There are two BMX racing cycles. One is a 20-inch wheel cycle and the other is a 24-inch wheel cycle.

Gameplay

This game is a single lap, off-road sprint race. Various bumps, jumps and rollers are added to the track. The off-road tracks with these obstacles provide the perfect combination of racing and stunt opportunities.

Bicycle motocross race is facilitated by multiple regional and international bodies, who provide the rules and categorical classification.

BMX racing is an individual sport. However, some races are done in teams.

Rules

On certain paths, the track is flat and has banked corners. Since the sport is open to different age groups, each age group follows a separate set of rules.

The rules usually pertain to the conducts of carrying out aerial skills and stunts. The riders in this game age from 2 years to 70 years. There are two jumping methods in this game—small roller and step up doubles.

Step up doubles

The step up doubles are bigger and up to 12 m in height. The starting hill marks the point at which the race begins.

The races are held on tall hills because it is usually believed that the taller the hill, the faster the race. Tall hills are for higher and more experienced age groups.

The step ups races are carried out on a combination of short and tall hills. They are named as "step ups" to provide the speed needed to climb the larger hill. Berms are the turns which allow the bikers to lean and turn at an angle. This lets them continue at their speed rather than reducing it to make the turn.

Doubles are two hills placed close to each other. Step downs are big hills, followed by the shorter ones. Rollers are known as the small hills in groups. There are different associations who decide the rules for the competitions. But the basic rules are applied to all the variants.

There are certain changes in the track length and difficulty of obstacles, based on different age groups and competition levels. The competition is judged on the basis of the time taken to complete the track length along with the mandatory aerial moves.

While BMX racing is an individual sport, often different teams are formed based on different categories. This usually takes place for a non-competitive event or for organisational purposes.

This is the first round in a BMX racing competition. The participants are jumping down to the shorter hill.

Wall of fame

Jim Pratt is a famous cyclist who performs jump stunts. In 1980, jumped over four cars in one jump.

R.L. Osborne jumped through a ring of fire. Later, many tried to copy this stunt.

American BMX player David "Dave" Mirra is a vert ramp and park rider.

Fact card

- The Wright brothers, who invented the aeroplane, used to originally run a cycle repair shop together.
- Over half a billion people in China own bicycles.
- The first person to have done a backflip on a bicycle had done it during a race. He did not win despite the awesome stunt. He secured the tenth position.
- A flat jump is a learning jump.

Dirt Jumping

Dirt jumping is considered to be the best stunt sport on a bicycle. The aim of this sport is to perform a jump, and land safely and gracefully after the performance.

Origin

This sport has evolved with BMX cycling and is very similar to other stunt sports like mountain biking. Cyclists enjoy jumping off the dirt mountains.

Eventually, the rules of the sport changed. The criteria for winning were changed from who performed the fastest to who performed the best tricks. In official games, there are set stunts that the riders can perform.

Dirt jumping is a mixture of freestyle and mountain biking. Hence, the game we see today is packed with features of both the sports.

Cyclists turn and twist their cycles when they are at a height.

Gameplay

The game is focussed on performing various tricks. The objective of the game is to score more points by pulling off the best tricks possible and landing safely. The "double" jump is the most commonly performed trick.

There is a setup for the jump, called the "step up" and the "step down". The step up allows the rider to leap in the air to perform the stunt. The step down allows the safe landing of the player. The bigger the gap between the two, the bigger the leap.

Tabletops are common among the new sporting line. In this stunt, the riders perform a step up but land on a flat surface. They need to have incredible control of their cycle for this stunt. Ski jumps only have a take-off. However, the stunt is longer and is performed on a flat surface.

"Spine" is a steep dirt jump with no specific tabletop to land on. It is meant for a high and distant jump. There are other variations like hip jumps, triple jumps, 360 beam jumps, etc.

This cyclist is performing the step down and is steering his cycle for a safe landing.

The riders need to control their cycles even in the air to ensure they land properly.

Fact card

- Mike Metzger performed the first Moto X backflip. It is a popular dirt jumping trick.

Downhill Cycling

Downhill biking is a fun sport where cyclists ride down slopes and drops. The cyclists seem to be racing against gravity in order to complete the course.

Origin

The first official record of this sport was set in Fairfax, California, on 21st October, 1976. During this time, cruiser cycles were the most popular cycles used for stunts. They had drum brakes, which needed to be pedalled backwards.

In 1979, mountain cycle companies improved the design and created the modern cycles that we see today. By 1990, the game reached its peak and the first mountain biking competition was held.

The game is very diverse in nature, due to geographical conditions being different in different countries. Hence, it creates a different set of rules for competitions, depending on the venue and availability. This makes the sport very interesting, as championship venues call for different training and specialisations.

Downhill mountain racing is an adventure sport because of the amount of danger involved.

Rules

As the sport is very rough in nature, its rules are centred around safety.

The cycles need to be checked prior to the race. Working brakes are a must. The performance must meet certain criteria.

All cyclists must wear protective headgear and padding. There is a speed limit set to ensure the safety of all participants. The weight of the cycles are also set. Downhill cycles are heavier, and feature front and rear suspension.

The design of the downhill cycle is such that it can smoothly glide on tree roots and small rocks.

Downhill cycling has different race formats. Depending on the formats, the players make single or double attempts to reach the finishing line as fast as possible.

The course for any race is defined by placing tapes on each side of the track. While racing, the players have to maintain their positions between the marked area. If a player leaves the course by crossing the tape line, he/she must return to the point of exit.

The stunts are not as important as the timely completion of the race.

Fact card

- The first bikes used were known as "klunkers" or paperboy cycles.

Freestyle BMX

Freestyle BMX is a stunt-based sport. It is classified as an extreme sport. It has to be performed on specific models of bicycles, known as BMX cycles.

Freestyle BMX is not as popular as the other types of cycling sports.

Origin

This sport was developed in the 1970s. Around this time, riding cycles in a park was a favourite pastime. Children would often have to pass through several obstacles in the parks. Groups of children would get together to perform stunts in parking lots or empty swimming pools present in the park.

Magazines began to publish pictures of these stunts. Soon this sport came to be known as freestyle BMX. It gained a lot of popularity. In the summer of 1978, entire parks were booked just for BMX cycling. The American Freestylers Association was formed within four years. By 1987, it became a popular sport worldwide.

Rules

There are no specific sets of rules to play the game. It majorly looks out for creativity and the combination of skills and moves. It has certain disciplines that are well established.

- **Street:** Public places are mostly used to perform these tricks and handrails, sledges, stairs, etc., are the main objects. This is one of the most common playgrounds for freestylers as it is easily available.

This form of cycling develops upper and lower body strength.

Fact card

- Most of the cycles look the same, but the make and features of the cycles are different as per the age group.
- A stunt where the cycle makes a 360-degree rotation is known as a "decade".

- **Park:** These are exclusive skate parks, where the focus is on ramps and transitions. They are commonly shared by skateboarders as well as scooter riders. They can be made of wood, steel or concrete. Concrete is used to build pools and bowls outdoors. It can withstand exposure to outside weather and crowd.
- **Vert:** It looks like a mini ramp. The ends are vertical and hence the name 'vert'. The riders can maintain their pace and speed during the competition. The vertical extension makes this possible. There are metal ridges at the end on the vertical lines covering it, which allow the players to grind. It also enables them to perform "lip-tricks".

Most freestyle stunts were developed by children.

Mountain Cycling

Mountain cycling is a sport in which cycles are ridden up or down a mountain slope. The terrains used in mountain biking are usually rough. The cycles used in these sports are especially designed to perform with endurance and durability. They are called "mountain cycles".

Origin

This sport tests a player's endurance. The first mountain cycle was created and then modified to use for long distance travel. In 1981, the Swiss military had made its first cycle regiment.

Cyclo-cross cyclists used to cycle to remain fit during winters. Groups were created to carry out off-terrain journeys. In 1966, the first special cycle was created, called the "mountain cycle".

This cyclist is riding his mountain cycle down a rocky slope.

Equipment & Gear

There are certain equipments and accessories that are essential for safety. The composition of cycles has changed according to the requirement. Gloves, glasses, shoes, hydration systems, GPS, navigation devices, pump and bike tools are the most essential equipment. In certain cases, even LED lights are attached to the bicycles so that cyclists can ride at night.

Protective gear is a must for this sport. Helmets, body armours and pads, first-aid kits and other requirements are mandatory. There are various cycles that are available according to the terrain. Cross country, all mountain endurance, downhill biking, four cross slam, free ride, dirt jumping, trails and urban cycles are some types of cycles used for mountain cycling.

There are different types of mountain bike races like cross country and short track cross country races. Stage races like bike trails, dirt jumping, etc., differ from country to country.

Injuries are a given when we consider the nature of the sport. The injuries can be minor bruises or major accidents.

This cyclist is riding his mountain cycle up a smooth slope.

The wheels of the cycles are strong enough to handle rough terrains. The cyclists make sure their position does not take too much stress while riding.

Fact card

- The first set of mountain bikers were named the "Buffalo Soldiers".
- "Derailleur" is the mechanism that is used to change the gears in mountain cycles.

Artistic Cycling

Artistic cycling is an indoor cycling sport. As the name suggests, it is not just about cycling but also about performing graceful stunts on the cycle.

Origin

This sport was invented in 1888. A few years later, the first artistic cycling world championship was held. It took place soon after an event where cyclists performed graceful stunts for the spectators. In 1956, the official world championship was held. It is an important milestone in this sport. The womens' official world championship was held the following year.

Rules

Participants must adhere to the rules with regard to the equipment which can be used and the costumes which can be worn. Each performance should be completed within the specified time limit. There are 5-minute performances done by individuals or teams.

The cycles which are used for performing stunts must have proper braking systems. Participants mostly use fixed gear cycles. Wheels are closely spaced next to each other in order to have a good balance and grip. These competitions usually take place in wooden courts.

A typical obstacle known as the bunny hop is used. Others include sand pits, planks and barriers. The normal regulation for any obstacle is 40 cm. The competitions are held for singles, pairs and teams with 4–6 people.

The riding area for artistic cycling is a wooden court, which has three concentric circles painted at the centre. Two areas of about 2 m are set. It must be free of all obstacles.

As in ballet performances, the cyclists must keep their feet and hands in graceful positions at all times.

In this stunt, the cyclists are holding onto the handles and supporting their entire body weight on their hands.

Artistic cycles are lightweight cycles that can easily be lifted into the air.

Fact card

- Most tricks from gymnastics are performed on these cycles. In fact, gymnasts who are good at cycling take up this sport.
- There was no true winner in the first tournament ever held. It was created in order to publicise the event. It caught the attention of the media and the common people alike.